GREAT MARQUES POSTER BOOK

JAGUAR

CHRIS HARVEY

WOODBURY PRESS

Contents

Introduction   4

1936 SS1 Airline   5   1962 Mark 2 3.8-litre   27

1939 SS Jaguar 100   7   1962 E type fixed-head   29

1949 XK120 lightweight   9   1965 E type roadster   31

1950 Mark V drophead   11   1968 420   33

1951 C type   13   1968 420G   35

1955 XK140 drophead   15   1968 XJ6   37

1955 Mark 1 2.4-litre   17   1972 E type V12 roadster   39

1955 D type   19   1976 XJ coupé   41

1958 Lister-Jaguar   21   1981 XJ12 HE   43

1959 Mark IX   23   1981 XJ-S HE   45

1960 XK150S coupé   25   1984 XJ-S competition   47

First published in 1985 by Octopus Books Limited, 59 Grosvenor Street, London W1

First published in the United States of America by Woodbury Press, One Corporate Center, 7505 Metro Boulevard, Minneapolis, Minnesota 55435.

Woodbury Press is the exclusive imprint of B. Dalton Booksellers, Minneapolis, Minnesota.

© 1985 Octopus Books Limited

ISBN 0 8300 0308 8

Produced by Mandarin Publishers Limited, 22a Westlands Road, Quarry Bay, Hong Kong

Printed in Hong Kong

Acknowledgements
Cars provided by BL Heritage/Jaguar Cars Ltd (pages 5 and 9), Nigel Dawes Collection (7 and 13), Classic Cars of Coventry/P.J. Masters (11), Alan Holdaway (15), Classic Cars of Coventry (1, 17, 23, 27 and 35), Midland Motor Museum (19), Bobby Bell/Bell and Colvill (21), John Blake (3, 25), Derek and Graham Bovet-White (29), Will Athawes (31), Gerry Margrave (33), Jaguar Cars Ltd (37, 43 and 45), Alan Hames (39), Roy Harris (41).

The publishers would like to thank LAT Photographic for permission to reproduce the photograph on page 47.

Page 1 Interior of a Jaguar Mark IX of 1959.
Page 3 1960 Jaguar XK150S.

Special photography: Ian Dawson and Chris Linton

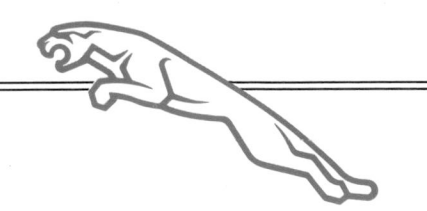

Introduction

From humble beginnings producing motorcycle sidecars in a seaside shed, the British firm Jaguar has risen to produce a vehicle acclaimed as the 'Best Car in the World': a stunning package combining performance, quality and value for money. But none of these qualities would have been enough for such an accolade had it not been for the cars' unmistakable style. They have almost invariably been the product of one man, William Lyons, knighted in 1956 for his services to British industry.

It was Lyons, with a partner, William Walmsley, who started the motorcycle sidecar coachbuilding firm at Blackpool in 1920. The name then was Swallow: a bird with all the grace and pace in the world. Lyons always favoured names from wild life to convey the message he created in metal.

The motorcycle combination was dealt a mortal blow by the introduction of the Austin Seven only two years after Lyons went into business; but no matter – he simply turned his attention to producing special Swallow bodies on the Baby Austin's chassis. He was not only a master stylist, but also a shrewd businessman, and an excellent production engineer who knew how to cut corners to save money without compromising on overall quality. As a result, Swallow bodies were leaders in cost as much as in style, and they became so popular that the firm had to move to Coventry, and ultimately to a much larger works in Browns Lane.

Lyons built bodies not only on the Austin Seven, but on other chassis made by firms like Standard. He gradually became frustrated at having to conform to the dictates of others, and he soon had Standard making special chassis just for Swallow. These cars became known by the name SS.

The SS1 was an immediate success and when its Standard engine was highly tuned for the classic SS100 sports car, Lyons had a machine that was a match for any.

But his main interest – and profit – lay in saloon cars, and his range of SS Jaguars produced in the '30s outshone even the products of M.G. Once again, he chose the name of a creature renowned for both speed and agility.

The letters SS had taken on a more sinister meaning by the end of the war in 1945, and so the cars became known simply as Jaguars. They were soon to be distinguished by an outstanding engine designed during the war and built in series in 1948: the XK, years ahead of its time as the world's first twin overhead camshaft hemispherical head production unit. Such sophistication had previously been the preserve of only the most exotic racing cars.

The reception that greeted it in 1948 was fantastic. The first mobile test bed, a sports car called the XK120, reached 212 km/h (132 mph) in mildly tuned form and created such a demand that it had to be put instantly into full production. It was an even bigger success in the car for which it was conceived, the Mark VII.

Then came Le Mans, the most important race in the world for car sales. Jaguar won no less than five times in the 1950s, to send the company's reputation even higher. Again, it was not just the fact that Jaguar won so many times, but the definitive way in which the cars won: three times in succession, with racing models the like of which has never been seen again.

The Jaguar D type was built like an aircraft and remains one of the most beautiful machines ever made. It certainly set a style of its own in 1954. This classic racer led to the breathtaking E type of 1961, whose super-streamlined contours caused another sensation: pop stars fell over themselves to buy the car, yet the price· was so keen that it was bought by ordinary people, too. Along with the Mini, the Jaguar E type was *the* car of that eventful decade. To cap it all, Lyons's compact saloon, the Jaguar Mark 2, was also welcomed with universal enthusiasm.

It only needed a combination of these last two cars to produce yet another great Jaguar: the XJ6, in 1968. This was the saloon that set the standard for Jaguar's competitors for years to come, and it was improved even more when Jaguar produced its second truly great engine, the world's first mass-produced 12-cylinder. Fittingly enough an XJ12 was voted the Best Car in the World in 1977.

By then Lyons had retired from active design in the company he founded, but he saw it revitalised 10 years later by a new chief, John Egan. Jaguar became a public company in 1984 – and there was a brand new range waiting in the wings.

1936 SS1 Airline

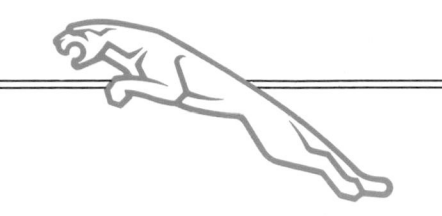

SS1 Airline

The SS1 Airline saloon represented the pinnacle of ambition for the aspiring owners of William Lyons's early cars. In keeping with the fashion of the times, it boasted wholly extravagent bodywork: Lyons, though, was not entirely satisfied with it, possibly because it was just what the market wanted, rather than a new creation. In essence, the Airline was like all the previous SS1s, the very first cars of the marque that was later to become Jaguar.

The initial SS1 in 1931 was a low, rakish, fixed-head coupé with the option of a 2054 or 2552 cc six-cylinder side-valve engine. At the same time, a smaller, four-cylinder coupé was introduced with a 1006 cc unit, called the SS2; but it was the SS1 that captured everyone's imagination because of its outstanding styling and relatively low price tag of just over £300. The chassis of the new car was made by Standard, who supplied the mechanical components, but it was available only on the SS, so the resultant product was a distinctive car in its own right, rather than just a special body on a chassis shared with another manufacturer.

Gradually, the SS1 was improved until it reached its final form in 1935 with the twin-carburettor Airline model. It was certainly one of the best-looking, if not the most practical, of all SS cars, even though its restricted headroom and fastback styling reflected something of a '30s craze. The interior of the Airline, with two comfortable seats at the front and two small ones at the back, showed one notable departure from the normal SS practice in that the seats were trimmed in plain, unpleated leather. This made it look much more modern than the earlier cars.

When viewed in retrospect, the early SS models performed only marginally better than rival cars of a similar engine capacity, and their owners had to pay substantially more for the privilege of having a faster-looking car. But the ultimate cost was kept within reasonable bounds by taking some well-disguised short cuts in construction. At the same time, the well-proven mechanical components from the mundane Standard saloons made the SS1, in particular, tough and reliable. This policy of offering exotic styling without the problems of an exotic temperament proved the ideal marketing package for Lyons's new company.

ENGINE		CHASSIS	
Type	In-line, water-cooled	Frame	Twin girders, cruciform bracing
No. of cylinders	6		
Bore/stroke mm	73 × 106	Wheelbase mm	3023
Displacement cc	2663	Track – front mm	1346
Valve operation	Side	Track – rear mm	1359
Sparkplugs per cyl.	1	Suspension – front	Half-elliptic springs, beam axle
Compression ratio	7:1		
Carburation	Two RAG carburettors	Suspension – rear	Half-elliptic springs, live axle
BHP	70 at 4000 rpm	Brakes	Drums front and rear
Transmission	Four-speed manual gearbox		
		PERFORMANCE	
		Maximum speed	129 km/h (80 mph)
		Fuel consumption	14.86 litres/100 km (19 mpg)

1939 SS Jaguar 100

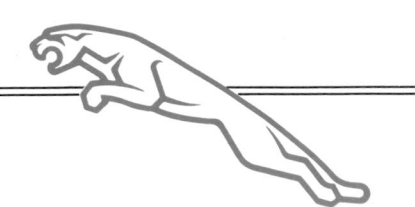

SS Jaguar 100

The success of Lyons's SS cars caused some people to snipe that they were not nearly so fast as they looked. Lyons did not wish these jealous accusations to be regarded as fact and decided to increase the power as soon as possible. He called in the brilliant freelance gasflow expert, Harry Weslake, who performed wonders on the larger 2.6-litre unit. Weslake produced an overhead valve conversion that raised the power output from 70 bhp to 105, with 125 to come from a larger 3.5-litre unit!

Lyons then went on to manufacture a lightweight short wheelbase version of the SS1, with the 2.6-litre engine that was called the SS90 because it was good for 90 mph. Lyons really excelled himself with the styling to produce one of the most spectacular sports cars made before the Second World War.

The latest engine was also used in a new series of saloon cars which were hardly less attractive. Such a new range also deserved a distinctive new name, and following consultations with advertising agents, Lyons called them Jaguars. These new SS Jaguars were a great success and when the 3.5-litre engine was fitted to the sports car it became known as the SS100 Jaguar in keeping with its new image and even higher performance. A smaller 1.8-litre unit was also offered in the saloon cars but was not used in the sports machines.

SS100s with their new-found power did well in competition, particularly a works-sponsored car driven by journalist Tommy Wisdom and magistrate Sammy Newsome. This car was frequently stripped for trackwork and soon became known as Old Number Eight, named after its chassis plate in the absence of number plates!

By the end of 1938, production was running at the rate of more than 5000 cars a year, although only a few hundred of these were sports machines. The time was ripe for expansion and Brooklands race-tuning ace Wally Hassan was taken on as chief experimental engineer, under a new chief engineer, William Heynes, from Humber. Lyons was already thinking of producing his own power unit with these key people to assist chief engine designer Claude Baily, Weslake staying on in a freelance capacity.

ENGINE		CHASSIS	
Type	In-line, water-cooled	Frame	Box-section girders, cruciform bracing
No. of cylinders	6		
Bore/stroke mm	82 × 110	Wheelbase mm	2642
Displacement cc	3485	Track – front mm	1334
Valve operation	Overhead, pushrod	Track – rear mm	1372
Sparkplugs per cyl.	1	Suspension – front	Half-elliptic springs, beam axle
Compression ratio	7.2:1		
Carburation	Two SU carburettors	Suspension – rear	Half-elliptic springs, live axle
BHP	125 at 4500 rpm		
Transmission	Four-speed manual gearbox	Brakes	Girling rod

PERFORMANCE	
Maximum speed	163 km/h (101 mph)
Fuel consumption	18.83 litres/100 km (15 mpg)

1949 Jaguar XK120 lightweight

Jaguar XK120 lightweight

Production of all SS cars ceased with the advent of war and the factory went over to aircraft and prototype work in 1939. During the latter years of the war, Lyons, Heynes, Hassan, Baily and new engine man Harry Mundy whiled away long hours, watching for fires on civil defence duty, by designing their revolutionary new engine. When the war finished in 1945, the initials SS – forever tainted by their association with Hitler's Nazi troops – were dropped to be replaced, quite simply, by Jaguar. The pre-war saloons were put back into production as part of Britain's export drive, with the SS100 dropped to avoid complication. One SS100, however, was assembled from parts for Lyons's son-in-law, Ian Appleyard, to drive with great success in international rallies.

Meanwhile the new engine was put into production in 1948. It was so advanced that it could not be made in large numbers immediately, so it was introduced in a new sports car, the XK120. This had a shortened version of a new chassis intended for Jaguar's major project, a completely new saloon, and a fantastic full-width body, even more pleasing than Lyons's earlier creations.

It was not anticipated that there would be great demand for a sports car in the austere post-war years, so the XK120 was manufactured initially with an aluminium body that was easier to beat out by hand and did not use the precious supplies of steel needed for export cars. Six of these new ultra-lightweight cars were provided for well-known competition drivers in the hope that their exploits would gain the maximum publicity for Jaguar.

They certainly did, with Appleyard and his wife Pat – Lyons's daughter – winning the Alpine Rally in 1950, 1951 and 1952 and the Tulip Rally in 1951 with one particularly famous example, registered NUB 120. Early XK120s continued to win races everywhere for years. A very pretty fixed-head version XK120 was produced from 1951 and a more luxurious version of the open sports two-seater, the drophead coupé, was introduced in 1953. The fixed-head coupé was not normally used in top-line racing because it was heavier than the roadster, but it offered all the comforts of a saloon car. The drophead coupé found popularity as an intermediate model between the open two-seater and the fixed-head.

ENGINE		CHASSIS	
Type	In-line, water-cooled	Frame	Box-section girders, cruciform bracing
No. of cylinders	6		
Bore/stroke mm	83 × 106	Wheelbase mm	2591
Displacement cc	3442	Track – front mm	1295
Valve operation	Twin overhead camshafts	Track – rear mm	1270
		Suspension – front	Independent wishbone and torsion bar
Sparkplugs per cyl.	1		
Compression ratio	9 : 1		
Carburation	Two SU carburettors	Suspension – rear	Half-elliptic springs, live axle
BHP	180 at 5300 rpm		
Transmission	Four-speed manual gearbox	Brakes	Lockheed hydraulic drums front and rear

PERFORMANCE	
Maximum speed	201 km/h (125 mph)
Fuel consumption	18.83 litres/100 km (15 mpg)

1950 Jaguar Mark V drophead

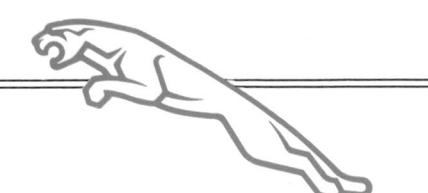

Jaguar Mark V drophead

Before the war, SS Jaguars had sold well abroad, so Lyons managed to secure sufficient steel for a new export drive in 1945. During this period, steel in Britain was rationed and available only to those who could sell their products overseas. Lyons was also able to buy the Standard tooling to continue production of the 2.6-litre and 3.5-litre coupés. The 1.8-litre unit was still available from Standard, so the post-war range was re-launched substantially as before, with engines in three capacities and a choice of saloon or drophead bodywork.

Left-hand-drive versions of these cars, known retrospectively as the Jaguar Mark IVs, were introduced in August 1947 with a special eye on the United States. Although they cost nearly twice as much as their pre-war equivalents, they were still cheap by post-war standards and sold well.

Meanwhile, Heynes and his staff had been busy developing the new engine and an ingenious independent front suspension system that took its inspiration from Citroën's famous *Traction Avant* of 1934. The wishbone and torsion bar design saved space and vastly improved the car's ride and handling. It also required a

revised chassis that had to be stiffer in order to perform at its best. This was duly developed with the intention of producing a completely new saloon car as soon as possible.

A new twin overhead camshaft hemi-head engine was designed for the new chassis – and saloon car – and made its debut in short wheelbase form in the XK120 sports car in 1948. The idea was to make a limited number of the sports cars so that they could be used for publicity and as mobile test beds, particularly for the planned new model. But there was not much, in fact, that could go wrong with the new chassis, so it was phased into production with its independent front suspension, and a handbuilt, pre-war style open or closed body, with the 2.5- or 3.5-litre engine, in 1948. It was the fifth of a series of prototypes, so the new car was called the Mark V to distinguish it from the superficially similar cars produced after the war, which adopted the Mark IV designation. These Mark V cars were only interim models on the way to the long-awaited new saloon car, but they performed well. One example driven by the Irishman, Cecil Vard, finished fifth in the Monte Carlo Rally as late as 1953: an astonishing performance.

ENGINE		CHASSIS	
Type	In-line, water-cooled	Frame	Box-section girders, cruciform bracing
No. of cylinders	6		
Bore/stroke mm	82 × 110	Wheelbase mm	3048
Displacement cc	3485	Track – front mm	1422
Valve operation	Overhead, pushrod	Track – rear mm	1422
Sparkplugs per cyl.	1	Suspension – front	Half-elliptic springs, beam axle
Compression ratio	6.75:1		
Carburation	Two SU carburettors	Suspension – rear	Half-elliptic springs, live axle
BHP	125 at 4250 rpm		
Transmission	Four-speed manual gearbox	Brakes	Drums front and rear

PERFORMANCE	
Maximum speed	134 km/h (83 mph)
Fuel consumption	15.69 litres/100 km (18 mpg)

1951 Jaguar C type

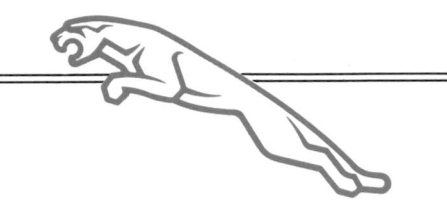

Jaguar C type

Such was the performance of the XK120 sports car at Le Mans in 1950 – when one example ran as high as third place – that Lyons authorized a special competition version aimed at winning the race in 1951; and because of the pressure of work on developing the new saloon for production, Heynes and his engineers found themselves with only six months in which to prepare the competition XK120 – the C type – before the great race in June. What they managed to achieve was incredible in view of the time available. The engine's power was increased by more than 30 per cent to 210 bhp, by means of a new high-compression cylinder head with bigger carburettors and a better exhaust. In addition, a new chassis was designed with torsion bar rear suspension, and the whole car was clothed in new bodywork. The chassis was very different from the XK120's, being made mainly from tubes to save weight without sacrificing rigidity. The rear suspension was designed with trailing links which gave better traction than the standard leaf spring arrangement. It was lighter and simpler than the popular de Dion racing rear suspension of similar layout and proved inferior only on bumpy roads; but as the C type was

designed solely to win at Le Mans, this did not matter, for the French circuit had an excellent smooth surface. The beautifully streamlined body reduced drag and featured a front end that lifted up in its entirety for quick and easy maintenance.

Le Mans was a glorious debut for the C type, with one example, driven by Peter Walker and Peter Whitehead hanging on to win, after teething troubles with the modified engine had eliminated two other Jaguars occupying the top placings. Jaguar was not content to sit back on its laurels and spent a lot of time developing a sensational new disc braking system. These new brakes overcame the problems associated with old-fashioned drum brakes: a tendency to overheat and lose efficiency when enclosed in the new all-enveloping streamlined bodywork. Overheating problems of a different type – caused by trying to over-streamline the front of the body – caused the retirement of all three C type Jaguars at Le Mans in 1952, but the following year they returned with a standard body shape and used their new disc brakes to the fullest effect to win convincingly from Ferrari. Rarely has a machine completed so hurriedly been so successful in such a demanding endurance race.

ENGINE		CHASSIS	
Type	In-line, water-cooled	Frame	Tubular construction
No. of cylinders	6	Wheelbase mm	2438
Bore/stroke mm	83 × 106	Track – front mm	1295
Displacement cc	3442	Track – rear mm	1295
Valve operation	Twin overhead camshafts	Suspension – front	Independent wishbone and torsion bar
Sparkplugs per cyl.	1		
Compression ratio	9:1	Suspension – rear	Torsion bar and trailing arms, live axle
Carburation	Two SU carburettors or three Weber 45DCOE	Brakes	Lockheed hydraulic drums or Dunlop discs front and rear
BHP	200 at 5800 rpm on SUs, 230 on Webers		
		PERFORMANCE	
Transmission	Four-speed manual gearbox	Maximum speed	230 km/h (143 mph) tested with SUs
		Fuel consumption	23.54 litres/100 km (12 mpg)

1955 Jaguar XK140 drophead

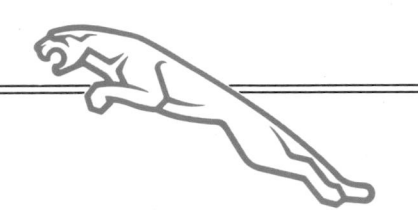

Jaguar XK140 drophead

The enormous expense of assembling the giant presses and tools needed for all-steel body construction of the XK120 could not at first be justified. But when it became apparent that there was a massive demand for the car this tooling work was set in motion – along with that for the new Mark VII saloon. Jaguar didn't have the capital to afford to build its own bodies by such methods, so the company had to wait its turn in the queue for outside contractors – with the result that both the all-steel mass-produced XK120 and the Mark VII could not be offered for sale until 1950. As soon as it was practical, the XK120 fixed-head coupé was introduced with a permanent steel top similar in shape to the roof of the new Mark VII. Wind-up windows replaced the original roadster's side-screens, the doors were fitted with exterior handles and the interior upholstered like the saloon, rather than the more spartan – and lighter – roadster. Ventilation had received special attention, with quarter lights front and rear, following complaints from people living in hot climates about too much heat in the cockpit. A heater was also fitted as standard, to counter complaints from people living in cold climates! These additional features were then transferred to the drophead coupé, which was a fixed-head car with a snug, well-lined, folding hood.

Jaguar's engineers concentrated next on revising the XK120 range in the light of comments from their sales forces, particularly in those export markets which took most of the production. The result was the XK140 of 1954, which used the same outer body pressings as the XK120, although the construction details were very different underneath.

The engine was moved forward 76 mm (3 in) to create more room in the cockpit and to improve weight distribution. An overdrive was offered as an option, and more precise rack-and-pinion steering developed for the C type was fitted. The rooflines of the fixed-head and drophead coupés were subtly altered and room found for two tiny rear seats, which made the car more appealing for families with small children. Stronger new bumpers like those used on the Mark VII were also fitted to ward off clumsy parkers and a more powerful engine, again similar to that used in the C type, was adopted so that the performance was not reduced by all the extra weight.

ENGINE		CHASSIS	
Type	In-line, water-cooled	**Frame**	Box-section girders, cruciform bracing
No. of cylinders	6		
Bore/stroke mm	83 × 106	**Wheelbase mm**	2591
Displacement cc	3442	**Track – front mm**	1308
Valve operation	Twin overhead camshafts	**Track – rear mm**	1308
		Suspension – front	Independent wishbone and torsion bar
Sparkplugs per cyl.	1		
Compression ratio	8:1		
Carburation	Two SU carburettors	**Suspension – rear**	Half-elliptic springs, live axle
BHP	190 at 5500 rpm		
Transmission	Four-speed manual gearbox	**Brakes**	Drums front and rear

PERFORMANCE	
Maximum speed	194 km/h (121 mph)
Fuel consumption	16.61 litres/100 km (17 mpg)

1955 Jaguar Mark 1 2.4-litre

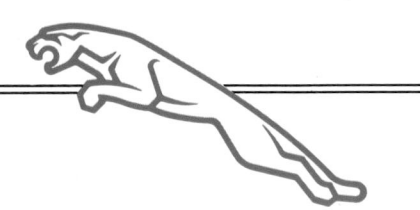

Jaguar Mark 1 2.4-litre

Although the XKs, which were essentially two-seater cars, and the Mark VII, which could accommodate six, were very popular, there was an even bigger demand for something in between. Jaguar therefore concentrated on designing a four-seater. Competition machinery aside, it was far more advanced in construction than the previous models. Jaguar decided to use a bodyshell of unitary design, although this needed even heavier investment than before in pressing tools. The new body – in which the basic shell doubled as the chassis – had a tremendous advantage in that it saved weight and was inherently more rigid. This was because the old-fashioned chassis, such as that used on the Mark VII saloon, was always a compromise. Weight had to be kept within reasonable bounds, so it could never have enough bracing to prevent it whipping, despite the changes made for the Mark V. This meant that the new independent suspension did not work to maximum efficiency.

The body, which was bolted to the chassis, helped to stiffen it, but not so much as a properly designed unit combining the functions of a chassis with the extra stiffening of a body.

Stress engineering for cars was in its infancy in the 1950s, so the bodyshell of the Jaguar Mark 1 (as it was designated retrospectively) tended to be, if anything, too strong and heavy; it was still a great advance, though. Very thick pillars were used to support the roof, which was an essential stressed component, and a sunroof was never fitted as standard (although the bigger saloons had them). As it happened, the new bodyshell was so stiff that it was not seriously weakened by cutting a hole in the top for a sunroof, so this feature became a popular non-standard fitting. Jaguar was also concerned that the Mark 1 might be too noisy, as unitary construction bodyshells often acted like steel drums when noise and vibration were fed into them. For this reason, everything that might transmit either noise or vibration was attached to the bodyshell by rubber blocks.

With such a stiff basis to the car, relatively soft suspension could be used, which paid dividends in both ride and roadholding. Economy was thought to be an attractive feature in a medium-sized saloon car, so the Mark 1 was fitted with a 2.4-litre version of the XK engine on introduction in 1955 – although larger and more powerful variants of this engine were soon offered for those who demanded maximum performance.

ENGINE				CHASSIS	
Type	In-line, water-cooled			**Frame**	Unitary construction
No. of cylinders	6			**Wheelbase mm**	2677
Bore/stroke mm	83 × 76.5			**Track – front mm**	1387
Displacement cc	2483			**Track – rear mm**	1273
Valve operation	Twin overhead camshafts			**Suspension – front**	Independent wishbone and coil
Sparkplugs per cyl.	1			**Suspension – rear**	Half-elliptic springs, live axle, cantilever, Panhard rod
Compression ratio	8:1				
Carburation	Two Solex carburettors			**Brakes**	Dunlop discs front and rear
BHP	112 at 5750 rpm				
Transmission	Four-speed manual gearbox			**PERFORMANCE**	
				Maximum speed	163 km/h (101 mph)
				Fuel consumption	14.87 litres/100 km (19 mpg)

1955 Jaguar D type

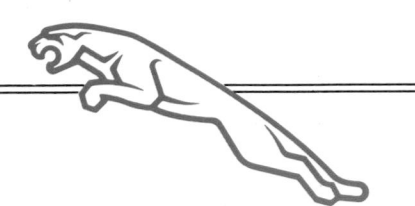

Jaguar D type

The D type Jaguar is the most famous machine ever made by the Coventry firm, not only because it was Jaguar's most successful racer, but also because of its sheer beauty. The extraordinary shape was based on that of contemporary aircraft practice, as was much of its construction. The fuselage-like centre section, called a monocoque, contained the driver and controls, with the fuel tank in the rear. The engine, transmission and front suspension were supported by a separate sub-frame, with the entire front of the car lifting up for quick maintenance, like its predecessor, the C type. In this way the D type represented a competition form of the soon-to-be introduced Mark 1's unitary bodyshell. At first the 3.4-litre XK engine was used in its most highly tuned form in 1954, with the capacity being increased to 3.8 litres later. In some events on long, fast circuits such as Le Mans, an aircraft-style fin was fitted to the rear for improved directional stability. Later versions of the D type, used initially by the works team, had a longer nose for even better air penetration.

In its first race, at Le Mans in 1954, the D type showed itself to be capable of 274 km/h (170 mph) – 32 km/h (20 mph) faster than the C type – as it battled for the lead with a massive 4.9-litre Ferrari. The Ferrari won by a very short head, but after that D types won everywhere, especially when they went into production in 1955.

Le Mans fell to a works long-nose example that year for Jaguar's third victory in this highly prestigious event. The factory then concentrated on developing fuel injection in place of carburation for extra power and won again at Le Mans in 1956!

The winning car had not been entered by the works team, however, but by one of its customers, the Scottish team Ecurie Ecosse. It was at this point that Jaguar decided to concentrate the energies of its small team of highly skilled engineers on production cars and handed over the works D types to the Ecurie Ecosse to continue racing. The American privateer, Briggs Cunningham, also raced works Jaguars, with one D type finishing third at Sebring in 1957 – but the Ecurie Ecosse astounded everybody by winning at Le Mans again in 1957 for a historic hat-trick with one of their D types!

ENGINE		CHASSIS	
Type	In-line, water-cooled	Frame	Monocoque with subframe
No. of cylinders	6		
Bore/stroke mm	83 × 106	Wheelbase mm	2302
Displacement cc	3442	Track – front mm	1270
Valve operation	Twin overhead camshafts	Track – rear mm	1219
		Suspension – front	Independent wishbone and torsion bar
Sparkplugs per cyl.	1		
Compression ratio	9:1		
Carburation	Three Weber 45DCOE carburettors	Suspension – rear	Live axle, trailing links, torsion bar
BHP	250 at 5750 rpm	Brakes	Dunlop discs front and rear
Transmission	Four-speed manual gearbox		
		PERFORMANCE	
		Maximum speed	274 km/h (170 mph)
		Fuel consumption	21.73 litres/100 km (13 mpg)

1958 Lister-Jaguar

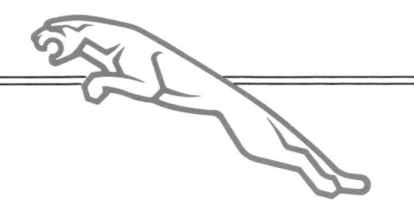

Lister-Jaguar

The D type was built specifically for endurance racing and tended to be rather heavy for short-distance events, so ultra-lightweight specials using Jaguar engines continued to be successful in 'sprint' races. In many cases, these cars had been developed from earlier versions using either 1.5-litre M.G. engines or a 2-litre Bristol power unit. Some of the most competitive specials of this type were produced by the Lister agricultural engineering firm in Cambridge.

One of its early cars, a privately owned example, was fitted with a C type Jaguar engine instead of its Bristol power unit as part of the quest for extra performance, and showed so much potential that it attracted the attention of BP, one of the oil companies who put up much of the money for motor racing at the time. They were keen to find a car to compete against the Ecurie Ecosse Jaguars and the works Aston Martins, which raced under the sponsorship of their chief rivals, Esso.

Although the constructor, Brian Lister, was not keen on using such a powerful unit as the Jaguar engine in his very light chassis, BP persuaded him to build the car. Jaguar was happy to supply a works D type engine and gearbox in the knowledge that it could provide formidable opposition for its rivals, Aston Martin. In fact, if it won, much of the glory would rub off on Jaguar, but if it lost it was probably because it was not a works car, just a Lister! Part of the attraction was that Lister also had an exceptionally fast and competitive works driver in Archie Scott-Brown.

In its earliest form, the works Lister-Jaguar used a tubular frame with coil spring suspension and a de Dion rear axle. In the interests of weight saving, the bodywork was kept to an absolute minimum, with lumps and bumps covering protruding mechanical items. It was christened Knobbly with good reason . . .

In Scott-Brown's hands, Lister-Jaguars dominated British sports car racing throughout the late 1950s, subsequent examples being fitted with more highly streamlined but bulbous bodywork designed by Frank Costin. Cars with both Knobbly and Costin bodies were sold to all manner of private owners, including Briggs Cunningham, who had a lot of success with them in America. In general the stark Knobbly Listers won more races and are remembered with greater affection.

ENGINE		CHASSIS	
Type	In-line, water-cooled	**Frame**	Twin tubes
No. of cylinders	6	**Wheelbase mm**	2303
Bore/stroke mm	87 × 106	**Track – front mm**	1321
Displacement cc	3781	**Track – rear mm**	1359
Valve operation	Twin overhead camshafts	**Suspension – front**	Independent wishbone and coil springs
Sparkplugs per cyl.	1		
Compression ratio	9:1	**Suspension – rear**	De Dion, trailing arms, coil springs
Carburation	Three Weber 45DCOE carburettors	**Brakes**	Girling discs front and rear
BHP	295 at 5750 rpm		
Transmission	Four-speed manual gearbox		
		PERFORMANCE	
		Maximum speed	274 km/h (170 mph)
		Fuel consumption	28.25 litres/100 km (10 mpg)

1959 Jaguar Mark IX

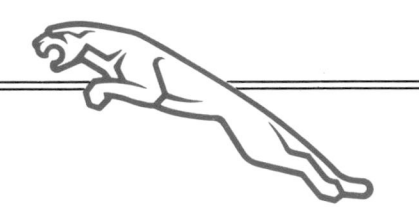

Jaguar Mark IX

The Mark VII saloon that was the Mark IX's predecessor laid the foundations of continuing prosperity for the Jaguar Car Company. It was the culmination of years of development and designed to sell in larger quantities than the XK sports car; although the XK achieved far greater popularity than had been anticipated, the Mark VII was still produced at the rate of about 100 per week against 60 or so for the XK. The reasons for the big saloon's success were threefold: it was extremely good looking, it could carry six people in great comfort, and it was very fast. The advertising men who launched the new saloon car range had no trouble in backing up their claim that it boasted unparalleled 'Grace, Space and Pace'.

William Lyons was at his most inspired when he designed the coachwork. It was a large car with voluptuous lines, but his talent for proportion made it also look graceful, even lithe. The chassis was the same as the Mark V saloon's except that the new XK engine was pushed further forward to make more room for the passengers. Mechanically, the Mark VII was similar to the XK120 except that its gearbox had more widely spaced ratios.

Like the XK, it was gradually developed in detail to accommodate market trends. By 1953, most Americans expected luxury cars to be fitted with automatic transmission. Rolls-Royce and Bentley were already offering this as an option, so Jaguar could not stand aloof, and promptly followed suit. In 1956 the engine power was increased, the automatic gearbox improved, and there was a certain amount of detailed re-styling, for a new model called the Mark VIII.

This had a relatively short production run before a visually similar Mark IX was introduced in 1958 with power steering as standard. This feature was especially popular in America where most big cars already offered it.

The Mark IX was also equipped with the 3.8-litre version of the XK engine and had disc brakes like those introduced on the XK sports car. This meant that its performance stayed well ahead of the transatlantic opposition. The Mark VIII, with its more economical 3.4-litre engine, was produced alongside the Mark IX until 1959. However, the Mark IX went on until late in 1961, when it was replaced by the first of a sophisticated new range of saloon cars, with all-independent suspension and unitary construction.

ENGINE		CHASSIS	
Type	In-line, water-cooled	**Frame**	Box-section girders, cruciform bracing
No. of cylinders	6		
Bore/stroke mm	87 × 106	**Wheelbase mm**	3048
Displacement cc	3781	**Track – front mm**	1422
Valve operation	Twin overhead camshafts	**Track – rear mm**	1461
		Suspension – front	Independent wishbone and torsion bar
Sparkplugs per cyl.	1		
Compression ratio	9:1		
Carburation	Two SU carburettors	**Suspension – rear**	Half-elliptic springs, live axle
BHP	210 at 5500 rpm		
Transmission	Automatic gearbox	**Brakes**	Girling hydraulic drums front and rear

PERFORMANCE	
Maximum speed	183 km/h (114 mph)
Fuel consumption	23.54 litres/100 km (12 mpg)

1960 Jaguar XK150S coupé

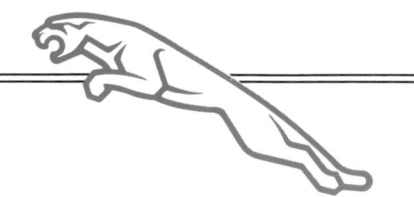

Jaguar XK150S coupé

Once the XK140 had been introduced, Jaguar's sports car range continued virtually unchanged as the factory concentrated on putting the Mark 1 and the Mark VIII into production. But automatic transmission was offered as an option on the slightly less sporting drophead and fixed-head versions of the XK140 in 1956.

Soon after, in May 1957, the XK was revised for the last time as the XK150. It was put on sale at first in drophead and fixed-head forms because the American market preferred a two-seater to an out and out sports car.

The body became bigger, heavier and more bulbous as a result and the engine was modified in line with the Mark VIII saloon to give it more torque in the middle range of its performance. However, almost as soon as the XK150 went into production, a serious factory fire caused extensive production difficulties. When the XK150 finally started to roll off the production line again, it had disc brakes front and rear – one of the first road cars to feature such advanced technology. As a result, although the XK150 was heavier than its predecessors, it was faster than they were on ordinary roads. The only real casualty of the fire from the XK enthusiast's point of view was a roadster version, which could not be brought into production until 1958.

This model had the familiar spartan interior and only two seats – but the drophead and fixed-head were much more luxurious in keeping with the saloons' trim, and they retained the tiny rear seats. The wider body and higher scuttle gave more room for the passengers and wrap-round windows were used to make the interior feel less restricted.

Later in 1958 the roadster was offered with a straight-port cylinder head and triple carburettors in 'S' type form, producing 250 bhp, to make it even faster than the earlier cars. These high performance options were then introduced on the fixed-head coupé, but not the drophead because that was intended purely as a touring car. Finally, in 1959, the 3.8-litre engine was offered on all models, with or without the S type options, to produce the ultimate development of the XK line, which continued in production until the end of 1960.

ENGINE		CHASSIS	
Type	In-line, water-cooled	**Frame**	Box-section girders, cruciform bracing
No. of cylinders	6		
Bore/stroke mm	87 × 106	**Wheelbase mm**	2591
Displacement cc	3781	**Track – front mm**	1302
Valve operation	Twin overhead camshafts	**Track – rear mm**	1302
		Suspension – front	Independent wishbone and torsion bar
Sparkplugs per cyl.	1		
Compression ratio	9 : 1		
Carburation	Three SU carburettors	**Suspension – rear**	Half-elliptic springs, live axle
BHP	265 at 5500 rpm	**Brakes**	Dunlop discs front and rear
Transmission	Four-speed manual gearbox		
		PERFORMANCE	
		Maximum speed	212 km/h (132 mph)
		Fuel consumption	18.83 litres/100 km (15 mpg)

1962 Jaguar Mark 2 3.8-litre

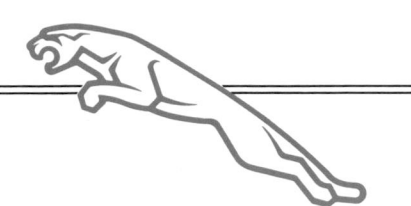

Jaguar Mark 2 3.8-litre

When the 3.4-litre engine was fitted to the Mark 1 saloon in 1957, with disc brakes to follow soon after, it was the start of seven years' dominance by Jaguar of saloon car racing. And when the Mark 1 was updated as the Mark 2, Jaguar found itself with one of the best-selling and most popular sporting saloon cars ever made.

Every aspect of the Mark 1 that had been previously criticized received attention on the Mark 2. The window area was enlarged by using slender roof supports, now that it had become evident that they were more thickly built than necessary on the Mark 1. The rather narrow rear axle was widened to improve stability, and the interior was restyled to suit contemporary taste, while maintaining Jaguar's traditional appeal.

All three engine capacities were offered with or without automatic transmission, and with overdrive as an option for the manual gearbox. Thus the 2.4-litre became the economy model, the 3.4-litre the middle of the range and the 3.8-litre – especially in manual form with wire wheels – the top performer, reaching speeds not far short of those attained by the XK150S, because the saloon weighed little more. The 3.8-litre model was also fitted with a limited-slip differential to make it even more surefooted on slippery surfaces. This was ideal for the racers, of course, although the vast majority of Mark 2s were sold to everyday users. Power-assisted steering was another option: it was especially popular in America. The system came in for criticism from some European customers who considered it too light, but the Americans, for whom it was intended, were well pleased. Because of their apparent lack of interest in economy cars at that time, only the 3.8-litre version of the Mark 2 was exported to the United States. It immediately established its reputation as an exclusive, ultra-high performance, medium-priced sports saloon.

In Europe, the 3.8-litre dominated saloon car racing from 1960 to 1964, taking over the mantle of the old 3.4-litre Mark 1, and only succumbing in 1964 to American cars with V8 engines of nearly twice the capacity. More than anything else, though, the Mark 2 became known as the Businessman's Express, because of its unique combination of comfort and performance. Ironically, it also established a reputation second to none as a getaway car in the hands of bank robbers!

ENGINE		CHASSIS	
Type	In-line, water-cooled	Frame	Unitary construction
No. of cylinders	6	Wheelbase mm	2727
Bore/stroke mm	87 × 106	Track – front mm	1397
Displacement cc	3781	Track – rear mm	1356
Valve operation	Twin overhead camshafts	Suspension – front	Independent wishbone and coil springs
Sparkplugs per cyl.	1		
Compression ratio	9:1	Suspension – rear	Half-elliptic springs, live axle, radius arms, Panhard rod
Carburation	Two SU carburettors		
BHP	220 at 5500 rpm		
Transmission	Four-speed manual, manual and overdrive, or automatic gearbox	Brakes	Discs front and rear
		PERFORMANCE	
		Maximum speed	201 km/h (125 mph)
		Fuel consumption	17.66 litres/100 km (16 mpg)

1962 Jaguar E type fixed-head

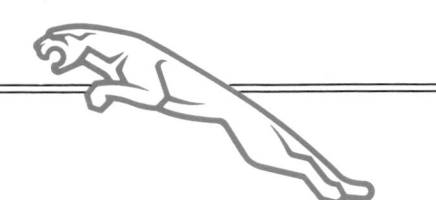

Jaguar E type fixed-head

The E type Jaguar that replaced the XK150 in 1961 caused a similar sensation as the original XK120 did in 1948. It was quite simply the most spectacular sports car available at that time to the general public. It was also far ahead of its competitors in that it was based on well-tried components that gave it a rugged reliability. The steel monocoque, which closely resembled that of the alloy D type in its roadster form, was also made with a sleek fixed head; the bonnet was similar to the one on the long-nosed D type with small bumpers reminiscent of those on the XK120, and later ones fitted to a few road-going versions of the D type, called the XKSS. The factory fire had killed hopes of more of these being made.

So the E type was the car that went into production. The XKSS had been produced in 1957 mainly to use up a surplus of D type spares. The E type's interior was lighter and simpler than that of the XK150, but the engine and gearbox were those of the 3.8-litre XK150S, except that there was insufficient room for the optional overdrive or an automatic transmission. Roadster versions of the E type were available with an optional hard top that followed established Jaguar lines – it looked rather like the roof on the XK150 fixed-head. The front suspension was mounted on a sub-frame bolted to the scuttle in the same way as on the later D types, and was traditional Jaguar in its wishbone and torsion bar layout. But the rear suspension was superior, as it was now independent to a wishbone and coil-spring format developed by William Heynes on a prototype called the E2A that raced at Le Mans in 1960, until eliminated with engine trouble. Wire wheels and disc brakes front and rear were fitted as standard on this rakishly impressive machine. Apart from its extraordinarily low basic price of £1600, what stuck in most people's minds was the fantastic performance – 240 km/h (150 mph) on road test with a 0–60 mph acceleration time of only 6.8 seconds, and a fuel consumption of 16.6 litres/100 km (17 mpg). Not only did the E type perform well and sell at a startlingly modest price, but it also looked far more attractive than any of its rivals.

It was no wonder that it became a cult car in the 1960s, along with the Mini. Just as the small British box on wheels established itself as one of the world's first truly classless cars, the E type rapidly created a clientele all of its own: pop stars and extrovert personalities certainly, but it was also cheap enough to be bought by people of average means with a taste for high style.

ENGINE		CHASSIS	
Type	In-line, water-cooled	**Frame**	Monocoque with subframe
No. of cylinders	6		
Bore/stroke mm	87 × 106	**Wheelbase mm**	2438
Displacement cc	3781	**Track – front mm**	1270
Valve operation	Twin overhead camshafts	**Track – rear mm**	1270
		Suspension – front	Independent wishbone and torsion bar
Sparkplugs per cyl.	1		
Compression ratio	9:1		
Carburation	Three SU carburettors	**Suspension – rear**	Independent wishbone and coil springs, radius arms
BHP	265 at 5500 rpm		
Transmission	Four-speed manual gearbox	**Brakes**	Discs front and rear
		PERFORMANCE	
		Maximum speed	241 km/h (150 mph)
		Fuel consumption	16.62 litres/100 km (17 mpg)

1965 Jaguar E type roadster

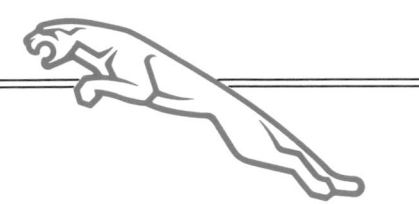

Jaguar E type roadster

To keep down the price of the E type it was necessary to use as many common components as possible with the big saloons which were still Jaguar's main source of income. Although these cars had a very high top speed, they were often judged by their acceleration times as American customers were intent on dominating their local traffic light grand prix. These customers, making up a substantial proportion of the total, had usually been brought up on automatic transmission as well. Although Jaguar's automatic gearboxes had become very sophisticated and smooth of necessity, they were at their best when linked to the immense, surging, torque delivered by a huge American V8. Jaguars were by no means deficient in the engine department, but it was decided to increase the capacity of the 3.8-litre engine to 4.2 litres, by using a bigger bore. In this form the new unit gave the same power, but seven per cent more torque – just where it was most needed in the middle of the range. Overall performance dropped slightly, however, because the new engine could not rev quite so fast with total reliability as the earlier 3.8 litre.

The E type had to use this 4.2-litre engine for economic reasons, but it made no significant difference, except in racing adaptations where revs were of paramount importance. But then the E type's days of glory in competition had been brief, because lightweight versions were soon outpaced by far more specialized machinery made in tiny numbers at a cost up to ten times as much.

In many respects, the 4.2-litre E type made between 1964 and 1967 was the most desirable of all models, with the lithe good looks of the original and a new all-synchromesh gearbox that was far more pleasant to use than the old XK120-based transmission.

The interior was also remodelled with more comfort in mind, later 'series 1½' examples featuring further changes to meet impending American safety legislation. This meant fitting recessed rocker switches in place of the old-style toggles and making deep cut-outs in the front wings for exposed headlights. These lights were not so pleasing aesthetically as the earlier, D type-inspired, fared-in headlights, but they were far more efficient for driving on a dark night!

ENGINE		CHASSIS	
Type	In-line, water-cooled	**Frame**	Monocoque with subframe
No. of cylinders	6		
Bore/stroke mm	92 × 106	**Wheelbase mm**	2438
Displacement cc	4235	**Track – front mm**	1270
Valve operation	Twin overhead camshafts	**Track – rear mm**	1270
		Suspension – front	Independent wishbone and torsion bar
Sparkplugs per cyl.	1		
Compression ratio	9:1		
Carburation	Three SU carburettors	**Suspension – rear**	Independent wishbone and coil springs, radius arms
BHP	256 at 5500 rpm		
Transmission	Four-speed manual gearbox	**Brakes**	Girling discs front and rear

PERFORMANCE	
Maximum speed	241 km/h (150 mph)
Fuel consumption	17.66 litres/100 km (16 mpg)

1968 Jaguar 420

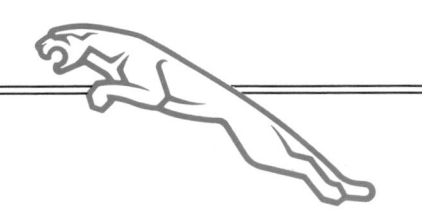

Jaguar 420

During the 1960s there was a growing demand for an even more well-appointed version of the Mark 2 saloon, inspired by the introduction of the vast six-seater Jaguar Mark X in 1961. It was not surprising, therefore, that Sir William Lyons decided to combine as soon as possible the more luxurious aspects of the Mark X with the established features of the Mark 2. The result was the Jaguar S type saloon introduced in 3.4-litre and 3.8-litre forms in 1963. These cars were of similar proportions to the Mark 2 and used much of the same running gear, but had the new independent rear suspension which had made its debut on the Mark X and the E type two years earlier. This rear suspension not only improved the handling, but the ride as well. The roofline was changed slightly to give more headroom at the back, and the rear bodywork was extended in an elegant manner to provide more luggage space – a vital factor for American sales. The interior was even more sumptuously appointed, and the frontal aspect was tidied up with new slim-line bumpers of a similar pattern to those used on the Mark X and E type. These new models were a great success (the Mark 2 continuing virtually unchanged) but they were not used in competition because they were heavier. Soon after their introduction, the manual versions received the new all-synchromesh gearbox that was to appear in the Mark X and the E type in 1964 and the Mark 2 in 1966 when sufficient supplies were available.

Lyons's next step was to ring the changes once again by fitting the 4.2-litre engine in twin-carburettor form into the S type to produce the Jaguar 420 – which was an immediate success as a truly luxurious compact saloon. This model, introduced in 1966, also had the front redesigned along the lines of the Mark X with a four-headlamp lighting system, but retained the original Mark 2 bonnet opening to save extensive re-tooling.

The old-established luxury car maker, Daimler, had been acquired by Jaguar in 1960, so a Daimler version was introduced at the same time, with the same engine, body and running gear, but with a fluted radiator grille, different badges and the name Sovereign.

The Mark 2 Jaguar saloons, and a Daimler V8 version, were then updated with the cheaper slim-line bumpers as the 240, 340 and V8-250 with 2.4-litre, 3.4-litre XK, and 2.5-litre V8 engines.

ENGINE		CHASSIS	
Type	In-line, water-cooled	**Frame**	Unitary construction
No. of cylinders	6	**Wheelbase mm**	2730
Bore/stroke mm	92.07 × 106	**Track – front mm**	1410
Displacement cc	4235	**Track – rear mm**	1384
Valve operation	Twin overhead camshafts	**Suspension – front**	Independent wishbone and coil springs
Sparkplugs per cyl.	1		
Compression ratio	9:1	**Suspension – rear**	Independent wishbone and coil springs, radius arms
Carburation	Two SU carburettors		
BHP	245 at 5500 rpm	**Brakes**	Discs front and rear
Transmission	Four-speed manual and overdrive, or automatic gearbox		
		PERFORMANCE	
		Maximum speed	198 km/h (123 mph)
		Fuel consumption	18.83 litres/100 km (15 mpg)

1968 Jaguar 420G

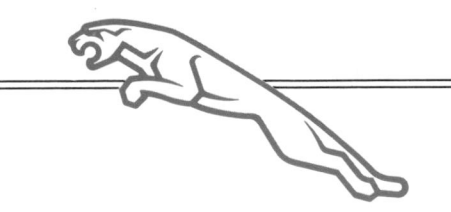

Jaguar 420G

Jaguar had high hopes for the Mark X when it was introduced in 1961 as a thoroughly modern replacement for the ageing Mark IX. It was the first of a new generation of Jaguar saloons and with accommodation for six people, sitting three abreast, was aimed squarely at the American market. In some respects it was similar to the E type sports car in that it used a wider version of the new independent rear suspension, with front suspension along the lines established by the compact saloons' wishbone-and-coil system. The rear suspension not only improved the new car's handling but it gave the rear-seat passengers a much better ride.

The Mark X used the same 265 bhp power unit as the E type because its engine bay was big enough to take the third carburettor. In fact, it was one of the widest cars ever made in Britain. It was also long and low, but the significant dimension was its width of 1930 mm (6 ft 4 in). Not only was the Mark X's body very large, but it was also exceptionally strong, being based on two massive box section sills – like the E type – with a steel floor pressing to connect them. But, unlike the E type, the front wings and engine bay were part of the structure, as on the contemporary Mark 2 saloon. The interior was similar to the Mark 2, except that it was even more luxurious and on a far larger scale. The Mark X's rear end was also redesigned to make the luggage boot – or trunk – extremely large, following the example of the Mark IX. This particularly pleased the American market. Unusually wide new wheels of only 14 inches diameter were used to fit in with its futuristic appearance.

Because of the power of the E type engine, the Mark X was still capable of nearly 193 km/h (120 mph) despite its great weight of 1880 kg (4144 lb). Extensive use was made of rubber-bonded mountings to keep down the road noise created by the very wide tyres specified for this advanced new saloon. The appearance was enhanced by its new slim-line bumpers and a four-headlamp lighting system. The engine bay and bonnet were so wide that there was speculation that it might be intended for use with Jaguar's new V12 engine, but that was not to be. The Mark X received the 4.2-litre unit in 1964 and became the 420G in 1966 to match in with the 420 – with the G standing for Grand to please Jaguar's American distributors.

ENGINE		CHASSIS	
Type	In-line, water-cooled	Frame	Unitary construction
No. of cylinders	6	Wheelbase mm	3048
Bore/stroke mm	92.07 × 106	Track – front mm	1473
Displacement cc	4235	Track – rear mm	1473
Valve operation	Twin overhead camshafts	Suspension – front	Independent wishbone and coil springs
Sparkplugs per cyl.	1		
Compression ratio	9:1	Suspension – rear	Independent wishbone and coil springs, radius arms
Carburation	Three SU carburettors		
BHP	265 at 5500 rpm	Brakes	Discs front and rear
Transmission	Four-speed manual and overdrive, or automatic gearbox	**PERFORMANCE**	
		Maximum speed	198 km/h (123 mph)
		Fuel consumption	20.18 litres/100 km (14 mpg)

1968 Jaguar XJ6

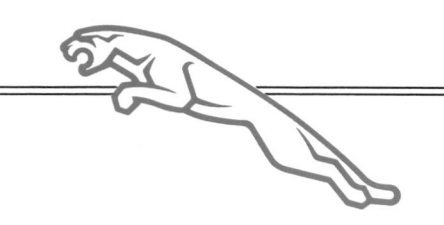

Jaguar XJ6

Jaguar's extraordinary range of saloon cars was rationalized in 1968 when all except the Daimler Sovereign and the 420G were replaced with a brilliant new car, the XJ6. It was a decade ahead of its time, establishing new standards in handling, comfort and silence without losing any of the established attributes of previous Jaguars, such as performance and value for money. Although it was a big car – slightly longer, wider and lower than the 420 from which it inherited much of its running gear – it was, in fact, based on the 420G. Its proportions were midway between the two, and, as such, it was one of the best-looking Jaguars. The body followed the 420G's massive form of construction with a wide engine bay and bonnet opening.

The new XJ6 (for six cylinders) was offered with either the existing 4.2-litre engine (still on two carburettors for economy) or an even more economical new 2.8-litre version of the XK unit. This was based on the earlier 2.4-litre engine, with a capacity of 2790 cc to take maximum advantage of European fiscal legislation. This unit could be revved much faster than the earlier XK engine because it had a bore and stroke of nearly equal proportions, rather

than a long stroke. It used the same cylinder head and carburettors as the 4.2-litre engine and produced 180 bhp, which was enough to propel this relatively heavy new car to 190 km/h (118 mph), with a 0–60 mph acceleration time of around 11 seconds. The 4.2-litre XJ6 was faster than the 420 because it had better aerodynamics.

The old team from Browns Lane showed that it had lost none of its touch with the XJ6. The lines were unmistakably those of Lyons, so much so that the name Jaguar was nowhere to be seen on the body because everybody knew it was the best of the 'Big Cats'! Heynes's superb engineering, particularly the suspension – which varied in detail from the 420 – made the XJ6 one of the quietest and best-handling cars in the world. The designers were so successful in their efforts to keep down road noise that they were able to use radial-ply tyres from the start, which improved the handling. This meant that Jaguar led Rolls-Royce by four years, because the Crewe firm were not able to fit radials until 1972, when it had redesigned the suspension. As a result, the Rolls-Royce Silver Shadow was simply not in the same class as an XJ6 for those years despite a price four times higher.

ENGINE		CHASSIS	
Type	In-line, water-cooled	Frame	Unitary construction
No. of cylinders	6	Wheelbase mm	2762
Bore/stroke mm	92 × 106	Track – front mm	1473
Displacement cc	4235	Track – rear mm	1486
Valve operation	Twin overhead camshafts	Suspension – front	Independent wishbone and coil springs
Sparkplugs per cyl.	1		
Compression ratio	9:1	Suspension – rear	Independent wishbone and coil springs, radius arms
Carburation	Two SU carburettors		
BHP	245 at 5500 rpm		
Transmission	Four-speed manual or automatic gearbox	Brakes	Girling discs front and rear
		PERFORMANCE	
		Maximum speed	204 km/h (127 mph)
		Fuel consumption	20.18 litres/100 km (14 mpg)

1972 Jaguar E type V12 roadster

Jaguar E type V12 roadster

Towards the middle of the E type's production run the wheelbase of the fixed-head model was stretched from 2438 mm (8 ft) to 2667 mm (8 ft 9 in) and the roof raised to make room for two tiny rear seats like those on the XK150. The longer wheelbase of this additional model, called the 2 plus 2, allowed the option of automatic transmission. The bulk and weight of the car reduced the top speed to around 210 km/h (130 mph) but it soon became popular with customers who needed more room, particularly in the United States.

More severe restrictions on exhaust emissions in America also forced changes to the XK engine which reduced power and made it run hotter. This meant that the nose had to be altered to provide a larger air intake for all models from 1968. These series two cars were slower than the originals but still far quicker than average because everyone else's products had suffered simultaneously. But the need for a new, more powerful engine was imperative if Jaguar's lead was to be maintained.

The company had in fact forseen these problems and started to design a new engine ten years earlier! This was the V12 unit that would be the equal of that used in any exotic car. The cylinder block, as well as the heads, was cast in alloy to keep the weight as close as possible to that of the cast iron XK engine. This meant that the suspension and bodyshells of existing cars would not have to be modified very much and the engine could be sited reasonably well forward to leave as much room as possible for passengers. The alloy block also dispersed heat very well, which had always been a problem within the confines of a Jaguar's sleek bonnet. But the original twin overhead camshaft cylinder heads on the V12 had to be replaced with single camshaft units to make the engine narrow enough to allow a decent steering lock when it was mounted in the front of a car.

Early single-cam V12 engines of 5.4-litres capacity (for maximum performance with reasonable fuel economy) were tried at first in a Mark X saloon, but introduced initially in the E type sports car in 1971 because – like the XK120 before it – it was in the most limited production. In this series three car, the longer wheelbase was standardized in both open and closed forms to produce more of a touring car, but with full original performance.

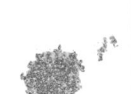

ENGINE		CHASSIS	
Type	V, water-cooled	Frame	Monocoque with subframe
No. of cylinders	12		
Bore/stroke mm	90 × 70	Wheelbase mm	2667
Displacement cc	5343	Track – front mm	1384
Valve operation	Single overhead camshaft	Track – rear mm	1346
		Suspension – front	Independent wishbone and torsion bar
Sparkplugs per cyl.	1		
Compression ratio	9:1		
Carburation	Four Zenith carburettors	Suspension – rear	Independent wishbone and coil springs, radius arms
BHP	272 at 5850 rpm		
Transmission	Four-speed manual or automatic gearbox	Brakes	Girling discs front and rear

PERFORMANCE	
Maximum speed	235 km/h (146 mph)
Fuel consumption	20.18 litres/100 km (14 mpg)

1976 Jaguar XJ coupé

Jaguar XJ coupé

American crash regulations were becoming increasingly demanding, and they led to the introduction of a series two version of the XJ saloon in 1973. The main differences between the earlier cars and the new models were in outward appearance and interior fittings. A new front bumper was located in a higher position to comply with laws that said that all bumpers should be at the same height. However laudable the aim, this was a waste of time for all concerned because in a crash the front of a car tends to be depressed by braking and the tail raised, so that the new bumpers missed each other anyway! Nevertheless, Jaguar managed to change the frontal appearance of its cars without making them unattractive, in stark constrast to the efforts of many rivals. The interior was completely revised making it more modern, with the instruments grouped in front of the driver, but it retained much of the old Jaguar 'walnut-and-leather' feeling. These changes (including recessed switches and crushable sun visors) were dictated not so much by a desire to modernize the interior as a need to meet the new safety regulations, which were far more sensible inside the car than outside.

The series two XJs were introduced alongside yet another variant, a two-door coupé. This model, which carried the suffix C (for coupé), was especially significant in that it represented Sir William Lyons's last project before his retirement from active design in 1972. The XJC used the original XJ6 floorpan rather than a longer wheelbase version which had been offered on the series two. It also had wider front doors and a slightly different roofline, but was otherwise substantially the same as the four-door saloons. However, there were a lot of problems with sealing the Airline-style rear windows, so the coupé did not go into production until 1975. Lyons had insisted on pillarless construction, which was very elegant, but posed innumerable problems for the development engineers who had to keep down the wind noise on these fast cars! When the cars were eventually introduced, the optional bodywork became available throughout the range, except on a Vanden Plas version of the Daimler, which was made in small quantities from 1973 to a higher standard of finish. The coupés also remained in relatively restricted production because of their short wheelbase floorpan; it had been dropped on the standard models by 1975 because everybody wanted the longer wheelbase, which gave more room in the back.

ENGINE		CHASSIS	
Type	In-line, water-cooled	**Frame**	Unitary construction
No. of cylinders	6	**Wheelbase mm**	2762
Bore/stroke mm	92.07 × 106	**Track – front mm**	1473
Displacement cc	4235	**Track – rear mm**	1473
Valve operation	Twin overhead camshafts	**Suspension – front**	Independent wishbone and coil springs
Sparkplugs per cyl.	1		
Compression ratio	9:1	**Suspension – rear**	Independent wishbone and coil springs, radius arms
Carburation	Two SU carburettors		
BHP	245 at 5500 rpm		
Transmission	Automatic gearbox	**Brakes**	Discs front and rear

PERFORMANCE	
Maximum speed	204 km/h (127 mph)
Fuel consumption	20.18 litres/100 km (14 mpg)

1981 Jaguar XJ12 HE

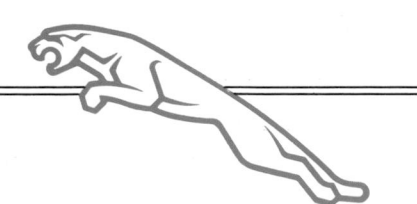

Jaguar XJ12 HE

The 12-cylinder engine transformed the XJ saloon when it was introduced in the first production model in 1972. Suddenly a superb high-speed saloon car became a full four-seater with a performance that more than matched almost any sports car. The top speed of 233 km/h (145 mph) and 0–60 mph acceleration time of only 7.4 seconds were breathtaking. This performance was also faster than the majority of grand touring cars, which had inferior accommodation and handling and often cost three times as much. The only disadvantage was that the XJ12, as the new car was called, used fuel at the rate of 23.54 litres/100 km (12 mpg), although this was not considered excessive at the time. It was fitted only with an automatic gearbox because of trouble finding an overdrive which could cope with its torque, and because there was no need for the extra performance that a manual gearbox would liberate. There was an immediate demand for the XJ12, even in countries where taxation and insurance were based on engine size. It proved the theory that if potential customers could afford to tax an XJ12 they could manage to pay for the fuel, an idea that was reinforced by a rapidly declining demand for the 2.8-litre car.

This was discontinued early in 1973, just before the world's great energy crisis. Suddenly the middle-of-the-range XJ6 became the most desirable model, as sales of the XJ12 fell. A 3.4-litre economy version was introduced, with the XJ12 continuing in limited production.

Petrol injection improved consumption, and, for those to whom such bills meant little, a Daimler Double Six Vanden Plas version of the XJ12 was acclaimed in 1977 as the Best Car in the World by *CAR* magazine after test comparisons with Rolls-Royce, Mercedes-Benz and Cadillac.

It remained substantially unaltered as a series three version was introduced in 1979 with a raised roofline to give more headroom and new bumpers to meet safety regulations. But work continued on making the engine more economical. Revolutionary new cylinder heads based on principles established by the Swiss engineer Michael May used a split-level combustion chamber to help improve the fuel consumption to around 13 litres/100 km (22 mpg) out of town. This new model was called the HE for high efficiency and restored XJ12 sales to a rewarding level.

ENGINE		CHASSIS	
Type	V, water-cooled	Frame	Unitary construction
No. of cylinders	12	Wheelbase mm	2864
Bore/stroke mm	90 × 70	Track – front mm	1270
Displacement cc	5343	Track – rear mm	1270
Valve operation	Single overhead camshaft	Suspension – front	Independent wishbone and coil springs
Sparkplugs per cyl.	1		
Compression ratio	12.5:1	Suspension – rear	Independent wishbone and coil springs, radius arms
Induction	Fuel injection		
BHP	299 at 5500 rpm		
Transmission	Automatic gearbox	Brakes	Discs front and rear

PERFORMANCE	
Maximum speed	233 km/h (145 mph)
Fuel consumption	20.18 litres/100 km (14 mpg)

1981 Jaguar XJ-S HE

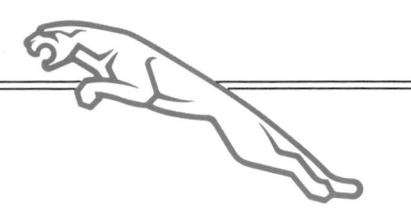

Jaguar XJ-S HE

The American safety and environmental campaigners had become so politically powerful by the late 1960s that sports car manufacturers realized that many of their vehicles would soon be outlawed as socially undesirable. This applied in particular to open cars, which were seen as particularly dangerous in a crash – regardless of the fact that many European machines had such good handling and braking that they were less likely to have an accident than many of their cumbersome American counterparts. The graceful nose of the E type and its underfloor-mounted tank were two of the items which would have had to be sacrificed to meet legislation that demanded among other things the ability to withstand collisions with huge concrete blocks. To have changed these features radically enough to meet the new regulations would have meant producing a new bodyshell, so it made more sense for Jaguar to make a completely new car. This would have to be a grand tourer if it was to use existing components such as the V12 engine, and made further sense when Jaguar saw the profits of Porsche in this field.

There seemed no hope of the Americans accepting an open car in the future, so the new Jaguar was designed as a fixed-head from the start. Unfortunately its bodyshell was virtually complete by the time American consumers rebelled against the safety lobby and won a test case allowing them to buy open cars – Jaguar just could not afford to start again at that point.

The new car's bodyshell was based on the XJ floorpan, with the wheelbase shortened to 2590 mm (8 ft 6 in) against the earlier 2764 mm (9 ft ¾ in) by moving the rear suspension forward and reducing the size of the rear seat pan. The front bulkhead and engine-bay sides were made as strong as possible. Huge 8 km/h (5 mph) impact-absorbing bumpers were constructed front and rear in a similar manner to the system adopted by Porsche. The new car's fuel tank was also moved forward to the front of the luggage compartment to protect it from possible impact.

Jaguar's four-speed manual gearbox was at first offered (without overdrive) for maximum performance in the new car, which was known as the XJ-S. It had the V12 engine from the start, and was updated in keeping with that of the XJ12 saloon to produce the ultimate XJ-S HE.

ENGINE		CHASSIS	
Type	V, water-cooled	**Frame**	Unitary construction
No. of cylinders	12	**Wheelbase mm**	2591
Bore/stroke mm	90 × 70	**Track – front mm**	1488
Displacement cc	5343	**Track – rear mm**	1473
Valve operation	Single overhead camshaft	**Suspension – front**	Independent wishbone and coil springs
Sparkplugs per cyl.	1		
Compression ratio	12.5:1	**Suspension – rear**	Independent wishbone and coil springs, radius arms
Induction	Fuel injection		
BHP	299 at 5500 rpm		
Transmission	Automatic gearbox	**Brakes**	Girling discs front and rear

PERFORMANCE	
Maximum speed	249 km/h (155 mph)
Fuel consumption	18.83 litres/100 km (15 mpg)

1984 Jaguar XJ-S competition

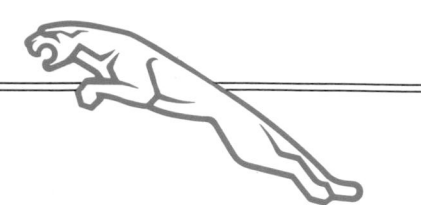

Jaguar XJ-S competition

Largely because of the energy crisis, Jaguar's sales were not as inspiring in the 1970s as they had been in the previous two decades. Consequently it was decided by their parent firm at the time, British Leyland, to return to international competition with a works team. The decision was taken in 1976, when the XJC was still in production, to use the coupé for an assault on the European Touring Car Challenge, which had given one of their rivals, BMW, a great deal of publicity and had been a happy hunting ground for the Mark 2 saloon in the early 1960s. The thinking was that the XJC more closely resembled the standard saloons than the lighter XJ-S, which could then be prepared in a more extensively modified form for sports car races such as Le Mans.

However, the XJC proved too heavy to survive the six-hour races which were the norm in the European Touring Car Challenge, despite a string of record laps testifying to the power that could be extracted from the V12 engine.

At the same time, the Group 44 team developed the XJ-S for racing in America. This was a different tale as the lighter car swept all before it in the late 1970s. Part of the reason for the failure of the XJC in European events and the success of the XJ-S in the United States was that the American events were shorter and the cars nearer to standard. The European rivals, such as BMW, were simply too highly developed for Jaguar to have instant success.

But the XJ-S's record in America did not go unnoticed as British Leyland withdrew the XJ coupé from competition. A private team run by Tom Walkinshaw realized that the XJ-S could win European Touring Car Challenge events in 1982 under new rules governing tyres and overall weight. Walkinshaw's confidence was justified as Jaguar XJ-S coupés, benefiting from Group 44 development, won four of the last six races in Europe that year. With full works backing for 1983, his cars came within an ace of winning the title, with five overall victories to BMW's six.

In 1984 there was no holding Walkinshaw. With seemingly endless energy, he managed his team, supervised the preparation, organized their season, and drove the leading car with former BMW star Hans Heyer. Walkinshaw had the satisfaction not only of winning the championship, but also of finishing first in four races and taking the drivers' title by ten points from Heyer!

ENGINE		CHASSIS	
Type	V, water-cooled	Frame	Unitary construction
No. of cylinders	12	Wheelbase mm	2591
Bore/stroke mm	90 × 70	Track – front mm	1488
Displacement cc	5343	Track – rear mm	1473
Valve operation	Single overhead camshaft	Suspension – front	Independent wishbone and coil springs
Sparkplugs per cyl.	1		
Compression ratio	9:1	Suspension – rear	Independent wishbone and coil springs, radius arms
Induction	Fuel injection		
BHP	350 at 5500 rpm		
Transmission	Four-speed manual gearbox	Brakes	Discs front and rear
		PERFORMANCE	
		Maximum speed	265 km/h (165 mph)
		Fuel consumption	28.25 litres/100 km (10 mpg)